Contents

Opening hours

Open every day except 24–26 December
Summer (mid-March to mid-October) opening hours
are 10am to 6pm
Winter opening hours are 10am to 4pm

For more information telephone 01223 835 000 or visit

iwm.org.uk

'...every individual, man or woman, sailor, soldier, airman or civilian who contributed, however obscurely, to the final result, may be able to find in these galleries an example or illustration of the sacrifice he made or the work he did'

Sir Alfred Mond, first Chairman of the Imperial War Museum, 1920

Introduction

Welcome to IWM Duxford. This former fighter airfield is a living piece of history which, during its 40 years as an operational RAF station, was home to thousands of young servicemen and women. During the Second World War in particular personnel from Britain, the Commonwealth and our Allies flew and fought from here. Duxford embodied the multinational mix of the Second World War Royal Air Force; with American, Belgian, Canadian, Czech, Polish and a host of other nations represented. Many did not return to their pre-war homes. There are lots of poignant reminders of their sacrifice, especially in the well-preserved historic buildings on site. You'll find on your visit that it's not difficult to imagine the scene in 1940 – or indeed at any other time during the war – as pilots such as the legendary Douglas Bader took to the skies.

As with many RAF stations, Duxford was continually updated and improved throughout its service life, and this process of development continued when the Imperial War Museum took over in the 1970s. The historic site has been augmented with modern purpose-built museum structures, including *AirSpace*: the story of British and Commonwealth aviation, the Lord Foster-designed *American Air Museum* in Britain, and *Land Warfare*. All these help us fulfil the museum's remit, ensuring that current and future generations understand the causes and, most importantly, the consequences of conflict.

As a five-branch family, IWM (Imperial War Museums) chronicles the impact of war during the twentieth and twenty-first centuries at all levels, and includes records of the experiences of men and women in the Armed Forces as well as civilians. At IWM Duxford, the focus is naturally on the world-renowned collection of aircraft and vehicles. The fact that on your visit you may have the opportunity to see one of the privately-owned historic aircraft flying from the airfield makes this site even more evocative.

Of the other branches of IWM, three are in London: HMS *Belfast*, our largest accessioned object; Churchill War Rooms, housed in the underground complex in Whitehall where Winston Churchill and his Cabinet met throughout the Second World War; and IWM London in Lambeth. The newest branch is IWM North in Manchester, housed in a building which represents a world torn apart by conflict, designed by Daniel Libeskind.

I would like to emphasise that IWM relies greatly on support of all kinds: from IWM Friends and our amazing teams of volunteers, through to those people who support us with donations and legacies. If you would like to help us, please visit our website for further details.

Thank you, and please visit us again soon.

Diane Lees
Director-General, IWM

Welcome to IWM Duxford. Perhaps best known as one of the world's leading aviation museums, we also have tanks, vehicles and naval exhibits on display. Our aims are simple: to preserve the exhibits that we hold in trust for the nation, and enrich people's understanding of the causes, course and consequences of war through a series of themed displays. In this respect, IWM Duxford is a series of museums in one.

AirSpace tells the story of British and Commonwealth aviation – both military and civil. In *Flying Aircraft*, our partner operators and private collectors maintain their airworthy aircraft. The regular flights of these 'warbirds' from the live airfield add immeasurably to IWM Duxford's unique 'living' atmosphere.

More flying aircraft can be seen in *Air and Sea*. This building also contains our maritime collection. *Battle of Britain* shows how the UK has been defended from air attack, and features more information on the history of Duxford itself.

Conservation in Action is where exhibits are preserved. Our conservation team is ably assisted in these tasks by a dedicated group of volunteers. They contribute to IWM Duxford's operation in many valuable ways. Our partner organisation, the Duxford Aviation Society, is also made up of volunteers that maintain the collection of civil aircraft that you can see in *AirSpace* and elsewhere on site.

The *American Air Museum* in Britain describes the development of US air power and the effect it has had on twentieth century history. *Land Warfare*, at the western end of the site, contains exciting dioramas and displays that chart the evolution of ground combat.

Historic Duxford is a new exhibition which tells the story of Duxford and its people, from the First World War to the Cold War. Duxford itself is made up of an extraordinarily well-preserved collection of airfield buildings dating back to 1917. The *1940 Operations Room* at the centre of the historic site is fitted out just as it was at the height of the Battle of Britain.

Finally, IWM Duxford is host to an array of spectacular, unforgettable events throughout the year. Visit our website regularly or sign up online to receive our email newsletter for the latest IWM news and more information on all our events and activities. I hope you make the most of your visit, and that you will continue to support us in the future.

Richard Ashton
Director, IWM Duxford

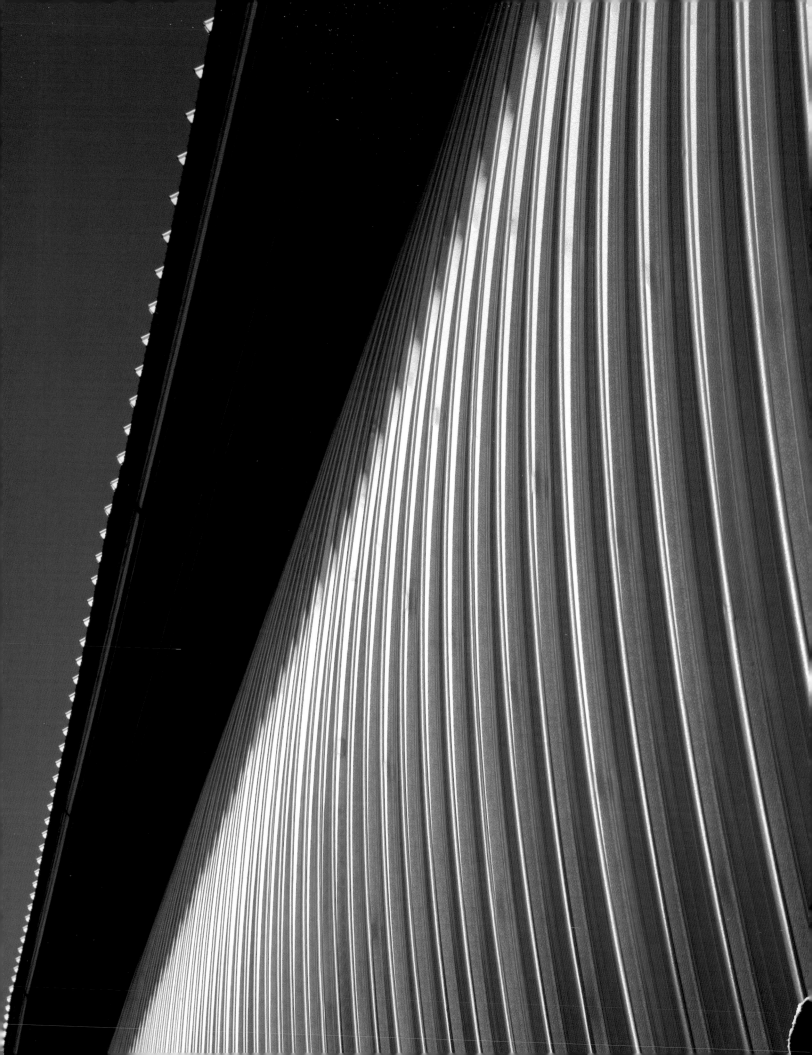

AirSpace

AirSpace is the story of British and Commonwealth aviation. Since the pioneering days of flight, Britain and the Commonwealth have played a major role in the field of aircraft development. The Aircraft Hall contains over 30 historic British and Commonwealth aircraft, including military and civil types. The Exhibitions Gallery is a fun and interactive family exhibition, with displays for all ages and all levels of interest. It provides an introduction both to the aircraft in *AirSpace*, and to some of the themes you can explore elsewhere at IWM Duxford.

Above Displays in the Exhibitions Gallery
IWM DUX_2007_030_010

The early years of aviation were shaped by British ideas and inventions. Sir George Cayley, arguably the 'father' of aviation, established many of the principles of flight that allowed so much development to follow. Other enlightened British engineers succeeded the American Wright brothers, refining and building upon their ideas.

Left and above The *AirSpace* Aircraft Hall
IWM DUX_2007_030_017
IWM DUX_2007_030_011

Above A Royal Flying Corps pilot studies his map (bottom right of picture)
IWM Q 54985

Above Applying 'Dope' to tighten the fabric on a wing in a First World War aircraft factory
IWM Q 28174

In 1912, the Royal Flying Corps was formed to take advantage of these new machines. It had military and naval wings whilst remaining part of the army. Soon, this organisation split. The military wing kept the name Royal Flying Corps (RFC) while the naval wing became the Royal Naval Air Service (RNAS). The First World War saw the expansion of both of these organisations. At the beginning of the conflict, it was felt by many in command that the prime use for aircraft would be reconnaissance, but it rapidly became clear that aircraft could also be used offensively. This led to the development of the bomber. Soon it was realised that armed aircraft would be needed to protect vulnerable reconnaissance aircraft and slow, heavy bombers. The fighting scout, later simply 'fighter', was born.

By the end of the First World War, Britain possessed the largest aircraft industry in the world: over 50,000 machines had been built. The technological advances made between 1914 and 1918 were huge, leading to the development of ever-more capable aircraft. 1918 also saw the amalgamation of the Royal Flying Corps and the Royal Naval Air Service into the Royal Air Force – the world's first independent air force, separate from army and navy control.

Airco/de Havilland DH9

The DH9 was one of Britain's first 'strategic bombers'. It was supposed to replace the Aircraft Manufacturing Company (Airco) DH4 in the Royal Flying Corps service. But the DH9 was fitted with an engine that was not powerful or reliable enough for the job. The DH9 was itself replaced by the DH9A, which had an improved engine.

After the First World War DH9s served with the air forces of many countries. Some versions were still in service in the mid 1930s. DH9s were also converted and used as air ambulances and passenger aeroplanes.

The DH9 in *AirSpace* was built by the furniture manufacturer Waring and Gillow of Hammersmith, London, in 1917. In the early 1930s it was one of three DH9s transferred under the Imperial Gift Scheme to Ganga Singhji, Maharaja of the State of Bikaner in western India.

Top The DH9 in its air ambulance role
IWM Q 69262

Above An Imperial Airways Armstrong Whitworth Argosy
British Airways Archive and Museum

By the 1920s, aircraft had proved their viability in several different roles. They were fighting machines, transports and reconnaissance tools. New records of distance, height and endurance were set and broken in the 1920s and 1930s, and aircraft proved ever more reliable.

The aircraft industry that exploded into existence during the First World War, including such illustrious names as Sopwith, A V Roe and Bristol, shrank in the post-war period, but development continued. New techniques, materials and processes were refined. A golden era of high-class and luxurious passenger travel emerged in the late 1920s, following the establishment of airlines such as Imperial Airways. The introduction of flying-boats meant that several new routes were opened to far-flung destinations, such as Egypt, South Africa and Australia.

The Second World War marked another giant leap in aviation development. Britain, as the focal point for the Empire and Commonwealth, welcomed over a million people into its flying armed forces.

Left A contingent of West Indian RAF volunteers on a troop-ship
IWM CH 13438

The success of the RAF in the Battle of Britain was crucial to the prevention of a Nazi invasion of Britain. As the war progressed, it honed its offensive capabilities to devastating effect, launching a strategic bombing campaign against Germany. Early efforts were discouraging – the accuracy of the bombers was poor, and the weight of bombs carried was not great. But thanks to improved navigation and target finding, better crew training and the introduction of heavy bombers such as the Avro Lancaster, RAF Bomber Command began to attack Germany night after night. Although some have argued that the campaign was morally unjustified because of the huge number of civilians killed – over 600,000 people as well as over 55,000 airmen – it nevertheless played an important part in the outcome of the war.

To meet the enormous demand for aircraft during the Second World War, the British aviation industry grew exponentially. At its peak, more people in Britain were employed in making aircraft than in agriculture and mining combined. Over 125,000 aircraft were produced. Women provided the backbone of this expansion, carrying out all of the jobs previously the preserve of men.

Avro Lancaster

The Lancaster was the most famous and successful British heavy bomber used by the Royal Air Force in the Second World War.

From their first operation in 1942 until the end of the war, Lancasters dropped more bombs than any other aircraft. They took part in every major night attack on Germany, and by May 1945, a total of 61 RAF Squadrons were equipped with them.

The Lancaster in *AirSpace* is a Mk X (Canadian-built Mk III). It was one of the 430 Lancasters built by the Victory Aircraft Company at Malton, Canada, in 1944.

Top Left The Second World War aircraft industry called on the skills of women as well as men
IWM CH 13693

Top Right The *AirSpace* Lancaster
IWM 2010_20_003_1

Bottom Left RAF Lancaster bombers during a raid over Hamburg
IWM C 3371

Bottom Right Ground personnel prepare a Lancaster for flight
IWM TR 188

Supermarine Spitfire

The Spitfire was operational on every front during the Second World War. The type has a strong association with Duxford, where the first operational Spitfire entered service in 1938.

The Spitfire remained in production throughout the war, being continuously improved to retain its superiority, with over 40 variants. When production ceased in 1949, over 22,000 had been built.

The Spitfire in *AirSpace* is an F24. This aircraft was one of only 80 F24s built. It was 160 km/h (100 mph) faster than the Mk I and could climb 3,300 m (10,000 ft) higher.

Avro York

The Avro York was developed in parallel with the Lancaster bomber, and the prototype first flew in 1942.

A total of 257 Yorks were built up to 1948. All the Yorks in RAF service took part in the delivery of supplies during the Berlin Airlift of 1948-49. The British Overseas Airways Corporation (BOAC) used Yorks for passenger services in the Middle East and Africa, until they were replaced by more up-to-date designs from 1950.

The York in *AirSpace* was delivered to the Royal Air Force in 1946. In 1954, it was sold to Dan-Air. During its career this aircraft flew the equivalent of 99 times around the world.

After the war, attention refocused on the potential of air travel. Wartime aircraft were quickly adapted to carry passengers. Turboprop passenger aeroplanes were introduced, then jet-powered airliners such as the de Havilland Comet. These aircraft dramatically reduced flight times, and with the introduction of pressurised cabins, made flying much more comfortable. As the post-Second World War period of rationing and austerity came to an end, more people found that they could travel abroad, and more businesses were prepared to pay for staff to travel in a burgeoning global economy.

Above Duxford's York in flight
Crown copyright, Air Historical Branch (RAF), Ministry of Defence

de Havilland Comet

British Overseas Airways Corporation (BOAC) launched the world's first passenger jet service in 1952, with Comet 1 aircraft. They cut flying times by half and were extremely popular with passengers, but by 1954, a series of disastrous accidents led to the grounding of all Comet 1s. Lengthy investigations showed the accidents were caused by metal fatigue, a little-known phenomenon at that time.

The Comet 4, developed from 1955, was of improved design and construction. It carried more passengers and had longer range. On 4 October 1958, two Comets, one eastbound and another westbound, made the first jet-powered passenger flights across the Atlantic.

Comet 4s continued to operate with some airlines until the late 1970s. The Comet in *AirSpace* made the record-setting eastbound trans-Atlantic flight on 4 October 1958.

Avro Vulcan

The Vulcan, originally conceived as a high altitude nuclear bomber, was the first four-engine aircraft to use the delta wing. The prototype flew in August 1952, and the Vulcan entered RAF service in February 1957.

The Vulcan served as a nuclear weapon platform for almost all its service life, armed initially with bombs and then in 1963 with the Blue Steel stand-off missile. However, it was with conventional weapons that the Vulcan first went to war, when it was used to bomb Port Stanley airfield during the Falklands War in 1982. The Vulcan in *AirSpace*, XJ 824, entered service with the RAF in 1961.

In the late 1940s, relations between the victorious Second World War allies broke down. The Soviet Union built up communist regimes in eastern Europe. Alongside the development of nuclear weapons, this was seen as a serious threat to the West. For over 50 years the East and the West fought a 'Cold War' based on conflicting ideologies and nuclear weapons technology. Fearing a Soviet attack, western European countries, led by the US, joined together in 1949 to form a defensive alliance, the North Atlantic Treaty Organisation (NATO). In response, the Soviet Union set up the Warsaw Pact of communist-controlled eastern European countries.

British military aircraft were effectively on the front line for the duration of this Cold War. Until the late 1960s, RAF 'V-bombers' – the Avro Vulcan, Handley Page Victor and Vickers Valiant, carried Britain's nuclear deterrent. The idea of this force was to discourage the Soviet Union from attacking, through fear of retaliation with nuclear weapons. In the late 1960s, British nuclear submarines carrying Polaris nuclear missiles took over this role. Throughout the tensions of the Cold War, British and Allied fighters and reconnaissance aircraft defended the skies over Britain and western Europe, ceaselessly guarding against sudden attack.

Above Left The Comet 4
IWM DUX_2007_011_004

Above RAF Vulcans and Victors painted in 'anti-flash' white
IWM RAF-T 5323

Airborne Assault

Airborne Assault tells the stories of the soldiers who go to war from the air. The Parachute Regiment and Airborne Forces played a central role in some of the most dramatic and heroic battles of the Second World War, including the Bruneval Raid, Normandy landings and the legendary operation to secure the bridge at Arnhem.

Airborne Assault traces the history of The Parachute Regiment and Airborne Forces from its inception to the present day, including operations in Afghanistan. Gain an insight into how today's highly trained paratroopers are at the heart of 16 Air Assault Brigade, the Army's rapid response force.

The story is told using imaginative displays of uniform and equipment, including medals, weapons and even 'Bing' – one of many 'ParaDogs' dropped into the battlefield.

Right Glider Pilots in the cockpit of a Horsa Glider

Far Right Inside Airborne Assault

Avro Canada CF100

The CF100 was the first combat aircraft of all-Canadian design. It fulfilled a demanding Royal Canadian Air Force specification for a long range, heavily armed, high performance night and all-weather fighter, able to operate from small Arctic airstrips.

CF100s entered service with the RCAF in 1953 and became the standard Canadian all-weather fighter, whose main role was to defend North America against a possible Soviet attack. Nearly 700 CF100s were built. The CF100 in *AirSpace* served with the Royal Canadian Air Force in Canada and Europe.

Above The Avro Canada CF100 was developed to defend NATO countries against attack by Soviet bombers
Courtesy of the Canadian Aviation Museum, Ottawa

English Electric Lightning

The Lightning single-seat, all-weather interceptor was the Royal Air Force's first supersonic fighter. The prototype flew in 1954 and was the first aircraft to exceed the speed of sound in level flight in Great Britain.

The Lightning could climb to over 18,000 m (60,000 ft), far higher than any previous RAF fighter, and was the main RAF fighter from 1960 until 1974, when the Phantom began to enter service. However, two Lightning squadrons remained on interceptor duties with RAF Strike Command into the 1980s. The Lightning in *AirSpace*, XM135, was the second production Lightning built.

Right The English Electric Lightning
IWM DUX_2004_053_006

The British aviation industry slimmed down dramatically in the 1960s, with firms merging to form new 'super' companies such as the British Aircraft Corporation. This huge new organisation was made up of English Electric Aviation Ltd, Vickers-Armstrong (Aircraft), the Bristol Aeroplane Company and Hunting Aircraft. The amalgamation took place after government pressure, and the rationale was simple: only by merging could the industry hope to cope with the financial and technological challenges of producing advanced aircraft. Although much development and innovation now occurred overseas, Britain was still capable of producing world-beating designs, such as Concorde (developed jointly with France).

'We all feel that it couldn't have come to a better place than Duxford'

Brian Trubshaw, Concorde test pilot, after delivering Concorde 101 to Duxford

BAC/Aerospatiale Concorde

In 1962, the British and French governments signed a treaty to develop a supersonic airliner. Though costs rose steeply, successive British and French governments stood by the project, producing an aircraft for the elite travel market.

Concorde went into service with British Airways and Air France in January 1976. Twenty aircraft were built in all: two prototypes (001 and 002), two pre-production (101 and 102) and 16 production passenger versions. The last scheduled flights by Concorde were made in 2003.

The Concorde in *AirSpace*, number 101, made its first flight in December 1971. It carried test equipment and was used to measure all aspects of the aircraft's structure and performance in flight. In 1974, it achieved the highest speed by any Concorde and made the fastest westerly civil trans-Atlantic flight, in 2 hours 56 minutes.

Left Concorde was one of the most recognisable passenger aeroplanes ever built
IWM DUX_2006_029_030

Above A Harrier GR3 on exercise
over Germany, 1976
IWM CT 78

Above The *AirSpace* Tornado, *Foxy Killer*, in service in the 1991 Gulf War. The Tornado multi-role combat aircraft was developed by Britain, Germany and Italy
IWM GLF 476

Hawker Siddeley Harrier

The Harrier was the world's first Vertical/Short Take-Off and Landing (V/STOL) aircraft. With no need for a runway the Harrier could take-off and land on unprepared ground close to battlefields.

The ability to take-off and land vertically was achieved by using a revolutionary jet engine with moveable nozzles to direct the jet thrust to different angles. The RAF's first Harriers entered service in 1969. In 1982, RAF Harriers saw service in the Falklands War, and more recently, in Kosovo. The Harrier in *AirSpace*, XZ133, served in the Falklands with No. 1 (Fighter) Squadron. During June 1982, it made at least 9 sorties from HMS *Hermes* and the forward airstrip at Port San Carlos.

Panavia Tornado

The Tornado was designed and built by a consortium of British, German and Italian aircraft manufacturing groups. It was designed to carry out strike, reconnaissance and interceptor duties in the air forces of all three countries.

RAF Tornados played a significant part in Operation Desert Storm, during the 1991 Gulf War. They were employed on the most dangerous missions of the campaign – low-level attacks on Iraqi runways against fierce anti-aircraft gunfire. They successfully repeated this type of mission in the Iraq War 2003.

The Tornado GR 1 in *AirSpace*, ZA465, served in the 1991 Gulf War. It flew 44 bombing missions, the highest number by any Tornado in that conflict.

Today, many modern, complex aircraft are built by global conglomerates – international companies coming together to develop a new machine. The European Airbus programme is a current civil example, but there have been several military aircraft built in this way – such as the Tornado, Jaguar and Eurofighter Typhoon. Most of these machines have to be multi-role too – gone are the automatic distinctions between, for example, fighters and bombers.

Aircraft are now an integral part of our lives. They are a vital part of Britain's military capability and allow us to travel vast distances easily. They have brought us many benefits. But the aviation industry faces many new challenges in the twenty-first century, not least of which is addressing its impact on the environment. Although there are bigger industrial producers of greenhouse gases, aviation is the fastest growing. Aircraft builders, fliers and airline passengers are beginning to take the threat posed by global warming very seriously. Even if this can be overcome, current aircraft are reliant on fossil fuels, a finite and diminishing resource. What will these issues mean for the future of air travel and the world of aviation?

Flying Aircraft

IWM Duxford's exhibitions are complemented by an active airfield. IWM does not fly any historic aircraft, but it works with several partner organisations that do. Many of their warbirds can be found in the *Flying Aircraft* exhibition. Here you can see these historic machines being maintained, repaired, or made ready for a new season of air shows.

Above The Red Arrows over IWM Duxford
IWM DUX_2013_028_015

Cambridgeshire County Council bought the airfield part of RAF Duxford in 1977; six years after the Imperial War Museum had begun using the site as a store. They opened it to private fliers, and since then it has been used by a variety of historic and modern aircraft. Today, the airfield is wholly owned by IWM. The original 1,960 m (6,430 ft) concrete runway was shortened by the construction of the M11 motorway and is currently 1,503 m (4,931 ft) in length.

During opening hours, a small team of Flight Information Service Officers, working from a Second World War control tower, provide Flight Information Services to pilots based at IWM Duxford, and to others flying in and out of the airfield.

The privately owned 'warbirds' based here are in frequent demand for air displays and filming work both in the UK and abroad. One of the largest and most famous aircraft to operate from the airfield is the Boeing B17 Flying Fortress *Sally B*, star of the film *Memphis Belle*.

Above Left The Consolidated Catalina operated by Plane Sailing. Photograph by Steve Crampton

Left The B17 *Sally B* delivers a breathtaking display
IWM DUX_2010_043_052

Duxford's role as a wartime fighter base is easily recalled when fighters such as the Supermarine Spitfire, North American P51 Mustang and Hawker Hurricane take to the air. They are owned and operated by the Old Flying Machine Company (OFMC), the Fighter Collection (TFC) and the Historic Aircraft Collection (HAC). Several naval and maritime aircraft are also represented, with examples of the Hellcat, Bearcat, Tigercat and Corsair belonging to the Fighter Collection. Other notable aircraft include the Consolidated Catalina operated by Plane Sailing.

If you visit in the summer months, you may see some of these aircraft being put through their paces in demonstration flights. During the winter, most undergo maintenance inside our hangars, to prepare them for another season of flying.

Air shows are staged regularly at IWM Duxford. Aircraft based at the airfield play a full part in these varied and exciting flying displays. Sometimes, they are joined by current military aircraft of the British and allied armed forces, as well as by civilian display teams and solo aerobatic performers. For the latest information about air shows, please visit iwm.org.uk.

Above Breitling Wingwalkers delighted the crowds at one of IWM Duxford's air shows in 2010

Left Not just historic aircraft: a parachute display team drops into an IWM Duxford air show
IWM DUX_2007_024_064

Top The Battle of Britain Memorial Flight
IWM DUX_2007_024_080

Above Left Spitfire display at The Jubilee
Air Show, 2012
IWM DUX_2012_044_386

Above Right A Grumman Hellcat
Photo courtesy of: © John M. Dibbs
- The Plane Picture Company

Left Visitors to IWM Duxford can take
pleasure flights in the de Havilland Tiger
Moths and Dragon Rapides operated by
Classic Wings (classic-wings.co.uk)
Richard Paver / Classic Wings

Historic Duxford

Duxford has been part of the Imperial War Museum since the 1970s, but its history dates back to the closing stages of the First World War. It achieved everlasting fame as the first RAF station to operate the Spitfire, for its role in the Battle of Britain and as a USAAF fighter base. Its story is now told in *Historic Duxford*, an exhibition which allows Duxford's veterans to share their experiences. They reveal what life was like at Duxford, a bustling community in times of war and peace.

Above Part of *Historic Duxford*, a recreation of the 1930s Watch Office
IWM_SITE_DUX 000980

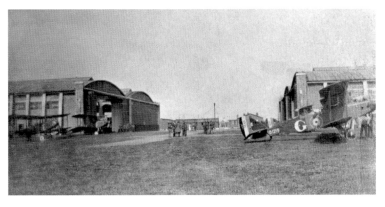

Above Duxford's hangars in 1918. The aircraft are DH9 bombers – one of the first types to serve at Duxford
IWM Q 114864

The site of the airfield was chosen in 1917 from farmland in the Parish of Duxford, approximately 11 km (6.8 m) south of the city of Cambridge. It was developed during 1917–1918 to become No. 35 Training Depot Station. Its purpose was to train new pilots for the Royal Air Force (RAF), formed in April 1918. One hundred and twenty-six pilots qualified before the end of the war, but there were 13 fatal training accidents – learning to fly during the First World War was extremely dangerous!

RAF Duxford was developed either side of the Royston to Newmarket Road (the current A505). Its domestic buildings including barracks and messes were to the north of the road, whilst the technical site with its hangars, workshops and airfield were to the south. This pattern of use continued throughout the station's operational life. A community of some 850 men and women lived and worked at Duxford during the First World War, including members of the US Air Service, who worked on the aircraft. An exceptional group of First World War technical buildings remain today. Among these are three 'Belfast Truss' hangars and the workshops and training buildings behind these, as well as the original MT (Motor Transport) Yard.

Above Pilots of No. 19 Squadron
beside one of their Gloster
Gauntlets in 1938
IWM HU 27835

Flying ceased in 1919 and the station was placed on Care and
Maintenance. It reopened in 1920 as the home of No. 2 Flying
Training School (FTS). Among the pilots trained at No. 2 FTS were
the famous aviation record breakers Jim Mollison and Charles
Scott. Duxford had links with Cambridge University throughout
the inter-war years. It was used as a base for research flying
and was the home of the Cambridge University Air Squadron
until the outbreak of the Second World War. Frank Whittle,
the inventor of the jet engine, often flew from Duxford while
he studied engineering at Cambridge in the 1930s.

The Air Defence of Great Britain was reorganised in 1923,
and Duxford became an operational fighter station in 1924,
a function that it carried out with distinction for 37 years. With
this came changes to the station, particularly in the 1930s as the
RAF expanded to meet the growing threat from Nazi Germany.
For example, a new **Guardroom** was built in 1933, a new **Station
Headquarters** opened in 1934 and changes were made to the
hangars to improve squadron facilities.

Duxford's fighters were directed into combat from the **Operations Room** in the **Operations Block**. This was opened in 1928, but was modified and extended in the late 1930s to accomodate new facilities. Before the war, air raid shelters were constructed to protect personnel, and the station was camouflaged. Later, on the grass airfield, 12 dispersed fighter 'pens' were built to protect the station's aircraft. The remains of one of these can be seen next to *Land Warfare*.

The squadron most associated with Duxford in the inter-war and early war years was No. 19. In 1936, No. 66 Squadron was formed out of C Flight of No. 19 Squadron. In 1938, these units became the first RAF squadrons to start re-equipping with the now legendary Supermarine Spitfire, a major change for the pilots. Prior to this, they were equipped with the Gloster Gauntlet. This was a 370 km/h (230 mph) biplane fighter armed with two machine guns. In contrast, the Spitfire was a sleek, all-metal, 586 km/h (364 mph) eight-gun fighter with a retractable undercarriage. The Spitfire entered RAF service reasonably quickly and with relatively few problems. During the Munich Crisis of September 1938, No. 19 Squadron possessed only three, yet by the end of the year the Gauntlets had been totally replaced by Spitfires.

Above Pilots of No. 19 Squadron in their room in what is now *Battle of Britain*, in the late 1930s
IWM HU 58243

Left Spitfires of No. 19 Squadron in front of what is now *Battle of Britain*, in May 1939
IWM HU 48148, courtesy of The 'Flight' Collection

With the outbreak of war in September 1939, expansion and rearmament barely came fast enough for the RAF. But in the summer of 1940, it made good use of its new Spitfires and Hawker Hurricanes in the Battle of Britain. During the Battle, Duxford was a sector station of No. 12 Group, Fighter Command and home of the 'Big Wing' of five squadrons led by Squadron Leader Douglas Bader. Among the squadrons that flew with the Wing were No. 19, No. 611, the Canadians of Bader's No. 242, the Czechs of No. 310 and the Poles of No. 302. The Wing played an important part in the Battle, particularly on 15 September when it successfully attacked a large number of German aircraft raiding London. The Wing of some 60 aircraft took to the air twice and was involved in a series of furious combats over southern England. Afterwards, the RAF claimed to have shot down 178 German aircraft, including 45 downed by the Wing. The number of claims bears witness to the scale of the fighting, but over-claiming in the heat of battle was common. Subsequent studies revealed that the Luftwaffe (German Air Force) lost only 56 aircraft. However, the scale of the defeat was sufficient to convince Hitler that an invasion of Britain in 1940 was not viable. 15 pilots lost their lives with units that either operated from Duxford or with the Wing during the Battle.

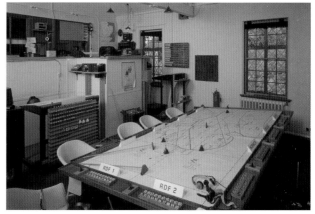

Top The Operations Room in 1940. The station's controllers directed Duxford's fighters into combat from this room during the Battle of Britain.
IWM CH 1401

Above The Operations Room reconstruction in the Operations Block
IWM_SITE_000332

Left Douglas Bader (fourth from right) with pilots of No. 242 Squadron at Duxford in 1940
IWM CH 1413

From 1940 to 1943, Duxford was the home of various specialist units as well as fighter squadrons. Among these was No. 5 Radio Maintenance Unit, whose job was to calibrate the secret radar stations that contributed so much to the British victory in the Battle. Also based here were the Enemy Aircraft Flight, which flew captured German aircraft, the Aircraft Gun Mounting Establishment, the Air Fighting Development Unit and even the Naval Air Fighting Development Unit.

The Hawker Typhoon entered service at Duxford in 1941, and after many difficulties, the first Typhoon Wing was formed at the Station in 1942. It flew in support of the ill-fated Dieppe Raid in August of that year. In this period the Station's defences grew with the addition of a ring of pillboxes. Off the airfield, the station sprouted a series of dispersed buildings and sites. Some were nothing more than groups of temporary Nissen huts, others were at large houses such as Sawston Hall, to which the Operations Room moved in 1941. In 1942, a new Watch Office was built to control the movement of aircraft on and around the airfield. Today, this building is known as the **Control Tower**. It replaced the 1920s **Watch Office**, which still exists next to the entrance to *Air and Sea*.

At the start of the war there were 15 military airfields in East Anglia. As the conflict progressed, the region's landscape became more and more militarised as new airfields were constructed. By the end of the war in 1945, there were over 120 in eastern and southern England. Many were built to accommodate the US Army Air Forces (USAAF), but in some instances the USAAF took over RAF stations. Duxford was one such base. In April 1943, Duxford became Base 357 of the US 8th Air Force and home to the 82nd, 83rd and 84th Fighter Squadrons (FS) of the 78th Fighter Group (FG). Duxford's facilities were so superior to those of many wartime USAAF bases that it was known as the 'Country Club of the ETO (European Theatre of Operations)'. But even these were not enough to accommodate all of the 1,500 US airmen who served at Duxford, and many temporary Nissen huts were added. Examples of Nissen huts can be found to the west of *Conservation in Action*.

'I loved the flying, because that was what I joined the air force to do, but there was a super bunch of people living in the mess. There was always a huge feeling of... camaraderie.'

Sir Dick Johns, Cold War pilot at Duxford

Above Luftwaffe reconnaissance photo of Duxford taken in 1940
IWM MH 26526

Above Captain Charles P 'Chuck' London of the 83rd FS, 78th FG sitting in the cockpit of his P47 Thunderbolt *El Jeepo*
IWM HU 57992

Right Colonel John D Landers' P51 Mustang *Big Beautiful Doll*. Landers was the 78th FG's last operational Commanding Officer at Duxford.
IWM HU 48197

The 78th FG was equipped with the P47 Thunderbolt and, from December 1944, the P51 Mustang. Its role was to escort US 8th Air Force bombers on daylight raids into occupied Europe and Germany, to destroy enemy fighters and to attack ground targets. In 1943 and 1944, US and other Allied fighter pilots successfully destroyed German fighter strength. Captain Charles London of the 78th's 83rd Squadron became the 8th's first official 'Ace', when he destroyed five enemy aircraft. On D-Day, 6 June 1944 (the long-awaited Allied invasion of Europe), every available 78th P47 provided cover for the Allied fleet as it crossed the Channel. Later, the group took part in raids on railway targets ahead of the ground forces. During the airborne landings in the Netherlands in September 1944, the 78th was awarded a Distinguished Unit Citation for the dangerous flak (anti-aircraft gun) suppression missions it carried out. Ground-attack or strafing missions of increasing length continued into 1945. By the end of April 1945, the 78th was flying six-hour missions to attack targets in eastern Germany. On 16 April, the 78th destroyed 135 aeroplanes on the ground and damaged another 89. This score was the highest ever achieved by an 8th Air Force unit, and a mission for which the group received its second unit citation. But these successes came at a cost: 113 American pilots lost their lives flying from Duxford – approximately the equivalent of the group's pilot strength. In October 1945, the Americans left Duxford, and the station was returned to the RAF.

After the Second World War, as international tension between East and West increased and grew into the Cold War, Duxford was updated again to face a new threat: Soviet bombers. The perforated steel plate that had been laid over the grass strip by the Americans during the war was not suitable for the new jet interceptor fighters of the 1950s. A new runway, 2,188 m (6,000 ft) long by 55 m (150 ft) wide, an 18 m (50 ft) wide perimeter track, and servicing and aircraft readiness platforms were laid, as well as 14 large concrete-walled protected fighter 'pens'. This completely changed the appearance of the airfield, but apart from the existing 1,503 m section (4,931 ft) of the runway, hardly any of this Cold War concrete now remains. The landscape looks much as it did in the inter-war period. Two large buildings were added to the technical site in the Cold War: a T2 hangar and an Armoury. Although the 1950s T2 hangar has gone, two others have been constructed on its site and now form the building known as *Flying Aircraft*. The Armoury has been converted into the Visitor Centre.

The Gloster Meteor was Duxford's first jet fighter. Meteors were replaced in the mid 1950s by the subsonic Gloster Javelins of No. 64 Squadron and the Hawker Hunters of No. 65 Squadron. The station, however, was regarded as unsuitable for the next generation of Cold War supersonic jet fighters, and the last operational RAF flight was made in July 1961.

Duxford's future was uncertain for several years. In 1968, the airfield was used as one of the locations for the film *The Battle of Britain*, when the smallest 1918 hangar was destroyed to simulate a German bombing raid. More damage was inflicted on the site during this filming than occurred in the actual Battle! By the early 1970s, much of the site was semi-derelict. The Imperial War Museum obtained permission to store aircraft on it, and with the help of a dedicated group of volunteers, the museum began to evolve. It has since grown into a world-class aviation heritage complex, the heart of which remains the preserved historic site of RAF Duxford.

Left A Gloster Javelin of No. 64 Squadron and Hawker Hunters of No. 65 Squadron over Duxford in May 1959
IWM HU 46501

Above Part of the *Historic Duxford* trail, showing the Station Headquarters building from which Duxford was commanded
IWM

The *Historic Duxford* Trail

Complementing the exhibition is a trail which will help you to understand more about Duxford's historic buildings and landscape. There are eight trail points dotted around the core of the historic site. Each one explains the activities that went on in that area, when Duxford was a thriving, operational RAF station. Each point also contains oral history recordings of Duxford's veterans, and historic photographs showing the airfield at different stages of its life.

Families can also pick up a trail leaflet in *Historic Duxford*, which contains a map showing the trail points. It's also an activity sheet, which children can complete as they follow the trail.

Air and Sea

Control of the sea is vital to an island nation. During the twentieth century, the method of asserting that control shifted from the giant battleships of the First World War to the submarines and aircraft carriers of today. The aircraft, boats and vehicles in the building called *Air and Sea* demonstrate how this change has taken place.

> '**Twenty aircraft inflicted more damage upon the Italian Fleet than was inflicted on the German High Seas Fleet in the daylight action at the Battle of Jutland**'
>
> Admiral of the Fleet Sir Andrew Cunningham on the Battle of Taranto

The huge surface warships of the First World War were designed to be the ultimate naval weapons. Equipped with large guns, capable of firing high-explosive shells over large distances, they represented the backbone of the Royal Navy and other nations' fleets. But even in that conflict, new weapons threatened the supremacy of these vessels. Arguably of most significance was the torpedo, carried by submarines and surface ships.

Above HMS *Dreadnought*. The large battleships of the First World War carried a huge amount of firepower, but were very vulnerable to torpedo attack

IWM Q 21183

Above HMS *Glory*. During the Second World War, aircraft carriers were often the most important ships in the fleet and gradually superseded the battleship

IWM FL 9455

Coastal Motor Boats (CMBs) were developed for the Royal Navy during the First World War. They were designed to attack large surface ships with torpedoes and operated mainly off the Dutch and Belgian coasts. After the war, several CMBs were sent by Britain to help White Russian forces in the Russian Civil War, which followed the revolution in 1917.

CMB 4 at IWM Duxford was one of two boats under the command of Lieutenant Augustus Agar RN. He used them on dangerous secret missions, ferrying spies into enemy territory. In June 1919, Lieutenant Agar carried out a daring attack on a Russian cruiser, the *Oleg*. For this successful operation, he was awarded the Victoria Cross. Because Agar was engaged in top-secret intelligence operations, the VC was not immediately made public. It became known as the 'Mystery VC'.

Motor Torpedo Boats (MTBs) of the Second World War were designed to creep into the enemy fleet, attack and escape at high speed. They carried two torpedoes and were fitted with two or three engines to maintain very high speed.

MTBs were used primarily in British coastal waters. They were often involved in high-speed battles with their German equivalents, Schnellboote (fast boats), known by the British as E-boats (enemy boats).

The vessel in *Air and Sea*, MTB71, is one of only four 60-foot Vosper MTBs built. It was commissioned in 1940 and served with the 11th MTB Flotilla at Dover and later the 1st Flotilla at Felixstowe, and was disposed of by the Royal Navy in 1945. In the late 1990s, after a long period in private ownership, it was obtained by the British Military Powerboat Trust and restored for static display. It was acquired by the Imperial War Museum and arrived at Duxford in April 2005.

By the Second World War, torpedoes fired by submarines and fast, mobile surface vessels constituted an enormous threat to any large surface ship. While Britain faced the threat of German U-boats in the Atlantic, Mediterranean and Arctic Seas, smaller surface vessels such as E-boats menaced British ships close to the coastline.

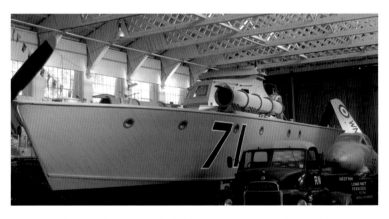

Above Augustus Agar VC
IWM Q 68014

Above Right MTB 71 in *Air and Sea*
Duxford Interpretation Department

Right Torpedoes being loaded
on to MTB70 at Felixstowe
IWM A 12909

The battle between submarines and surface vessels threatened to have a real impact on Britain's ability to wage war, particularly in the Atlantic. In 68 months around 2,000 Allied merchant ships were destroyed by U-boats, the vast majority carrying supplies vital to Britain's war effort. An arms race developed, in which new tactics and technologies were used to try to gain the decisive advantage. Eventually, what was known as the Battle of the Atlantic was won by the Allies, but at a great cost: tens of thousands of sailors lost their lives, including over 30,000 Merchant Navy seamen.

Above RAF reconnaissance photograph of the German battleship *Tirpitz*, lying in Tromso fjord, Norway. The *Tirpitz*, a piece of which can be found in *Air and Sea*, was considered to be such a threat to Allied shipping that repeated attempts were made to destroy it, using torpedoes, midget submarines and aircraft. Finally, in November 1944, Lancaster bombers of No. 9 and No. 617 Squadron damaged *Tirpitz* so badly that it capsized.
IWM C 5148 A

Left Although most associated with submarines and small surface vessels, torpedoes were also used by large warships. Japanese cruisers such as the *Atago*, pictured, carried Type 93 torpedoes, like the example in *Air and Sea*, during the Second World War.
IWM MH 6205

The silent and deadly menace of the submarine was soon matched by the threat from the air. The Second World War saw the increased effectiveness of maritime patrol aircraft and the coming of age of the aircraft carrier, equipped with aircraft able to strike at targets well beyond the reach of land-based aeroplanes. The Royal Navy's Fleet Air Arm played a vital role in several key operations, including the famous attack by Swordfish torpedo bombers on the Italian fleet at Taranto. This operation crippled the Italian naval presence in the Mediterranean. By the end of the Second World War, the aircraft carrier was the most important vessel in the fleet, and the large, ponderous battleship was almost obsolete.

Key developments in naval aviation in the 1950s included the use of jet aircraft. New methods had to be perfected to enable fast jet fighters to operate from carriers. For example, steam-powered catapults were used to provide the power necessary to launch a heavy jet. The Fleet Air Arm used its jet fighters, such as the Sea Hawk, in the Suez campaign of 1956.

> ## 'A loud explosion shook the ship, so I ordered the armoured hatch to be closed, thinking that bombs were again falling. Actually it was a torpedo somewhere amidships.'
>
> Lt Cmdr S G Hamilton RNVR, HMS *Repulse*,
> on the sinking of his ship

Below Fleet Air Arm Fairey Swordfish
IWM A 3532

Hawker Sea Hawk

The prototype Sea Hawk was Hawker's first jet aircraft. It proved to be very popular with its pilots, who spoke highly of its manoeuvrability and ease of control. Sea Hawks saw operational service with five squadrons embarked on the carriers HMS *Albion*, *Eagle* and *Bulwark* during the Suez campaign of 1956.

The Fleet Air Arm retired its Sea Hawks from front-line service in 1960, but the aircraft remained in service, notably with the West German Navy, which had ordered 64 of them in 1956. Other foreign purchasers were India and the Netherlands. Most Sea Hawks were built by Armstrong Siddeley, as Hawker was concentrating production on the Hunter fighter.

The helicopter was developed for naval purposes immediately after the Second World War and is today a vital naval weapon. It was initially used primarily for ship-to-shore communication and rescue duties. But as more powerful helicopters began to be introduced, their role expanded to anti-submarine missions and eventually troop-carrying.

Top A Hawker Sea Hawk about to be launched on an operation against Egyptian airfields during the Suez Crisis, 1956
IWM A 33616

Above Duxford's Buccaneer lands on HMS *Ark Royal*
IWM SFPU_AR_ 28435

Left Duxford's Wasp taking off from the deck of HMS *Apollo*
Courtesy of Stuart Reid

Westland Wasp

The Wasp was the naval version of the British Army's Scout helicopter. It was compact, light and could fly from a small hangar and flight deck on board anti-submarine frigates, patrol and survey ships.

Wasps on board HMS *Endurance*, an ice patrol ship that had made several voyages to the South Atlantic, attacked an Argentine submarine, the *Santa Fe*, just before South Georgia was recaptured by the British in April 1982.

Duxford's Wasp started service in 1964. It flew from HMS *Apollo*, which was part of the Falklands Task Force. It was retired in 1986.

Battle of Britain

Before the First World War, control of the sea by the Royal Navy prevented attacks on the United Kingdom. But during the war, the country was exposed to a new form of attack: from the air. For the first time, civilians found themselves in the front line alongside the military.

Between 1915 and 1918, German airships and bomber aircraft raided Britain. Although the damage and the number of deaths (1,368) was relatively small compared to the 60,000 killed by German raids during the Second World War, Britain responded by creating an air defence system.

From 1916, a network of observer posts was developed. They reported air raids by telephone to control rooms, which in turn directed searchlights, anti-aircraft guns and fighter aircraft to attack the bombers. Civilians were also given early warning of the raids so they could take shelter. This system was still being refined when German raids ceased, but it was re-adopted and updated before the Second World War with the introduction of modern communications, radar and new fighter aircraft to counter the threat from Nazi Germany.

Top Damage caused to buildings on Pancras Road, London, by a German Gotha bomber air raid in 1917
IWM HO 76

Above The Bristol F2B Fighter
IWM 2010_045_002_1

Bristol F2B Fighter

The Bristol Fighter was a First World War two-seat fighter. It became one of the most successful Allied aircraft on the Western Front in 1917 – 1918. The Bristol Fighter remained in RAF service after the war and was used by the Cambridge University Air Squadron at Duxford as late as 1931.

F2Bs equipped three Home Defence Squadrons. The Bristol Fighter in *Battle of Britain* was built in September 1918 and issued to No. 39 Home Defence Squadron, RAF, at North Weald, Essex.

The Second World War began in September 1939. The following spring, Germany invaded and occupied the Low Countries and France, and Hitler turned his attention to forcing Britain out of the war. To clear the way for an invasion, the Luftwaffe (German air force) had to win control of the skies over the UK. Only the Royal Air Force could prevent this. Despite 16 weeks of air fighting and bombing in what became known as the Battle of Britain, the Luftwaffe failed to destroy RAF Fighter Command. Hitler therefore postponed the invasion, and Britain remained in the war with its air force undefeated.

2,917 men were officially recognised as having taken part in the Battle of Britain. These were the men Churchill referred to as the 'Few'. Most of them were pilots in Fighter Command. Just over 10 per cent came from abroad, most of them from the Commonwealth or from occupied countries such as France, Belgium, Poland and Czechoslovakia. These men and their aircraft, especially the Spitfire, instantly became symbols of the freedom they helped to win. 544 airmen died in the Battle of Britain. 2,698 Luftwaffe aircrew also lost their lives.

In the early days of the battle, German bombing raids concentrated on RAF airfields. But the RAF managed to survive the onslaught. Then, the Luftwaffe turned its attention to British cities. They were raided every night, from September 1940 to May 1941, in a campaign known as 'the Blitz'. The aim was to break British morale by making production, transport and daily life impossible. London suffered the most. On the worst night, 10 May 1941, 1,436 civilians were killed. Clydeside near Glasgow took the biggest bombing relative to its size: after raids in January 1941, it was left with only seven of its 12,000 houses undamaged.

Hawker Hurricane Mk IIB

The Hurricane Mk I was the RAF's first single-seat 8-gun monoplane fighter. The Hurricane, rather than the more famous Spitfire, was the main British fighter in the Battle of Britain. Thirty-two RAF squadrons flew Hurricanes, 19 were equipped with Spitfires. In 1940, the Hurricane destroyed more enemy aircraft than all other defences combined.

The Hurricane Mk IIB in *Battle of Britain* was recovered from a crash site in Russia. The Mk IIB did not enter service until 1941 but this aircraft is painted to represent a Mk IIA of No. 111 Squadron in 1940.

Above Hawker Hurricanes of
No. 85 Squadron, October 1940
IWM CH 1500

Messerschmitt Bf109E

The Bf109 was the most famous German fighter of the Second World War. The aircraft in *Battle of Britain*, 1190, saw combat with the fighter unit JG26 in the Battles of France and Britain. It shot down five Allied aircraft but on 30 September 1940, its engine failed and the aircraft crash-landed in a field near East Dean, Sussex. The pilot, Horst Perez, was shot, wounded and captured.

In 1940, the Luftwaffe put over 1,000 of its excellent Bf109s into combat against the RAF. Their performance was better than the Hurricane's and only equalled by the Spitfire. However, the 109s lacked range, so they could not always stay in combat long enough or in sufficient numbers to defeat the RAF's fighters.

Above Duxford's Bf109E under guard at
its crash site in Sussex, September 1940
IWM HU 73139, courtesy of the *Eastbourne Gazette*

Fordson WOT 1 balloon winch

Large balloons of over 18.3 m (60 ft) fixed on wire cables were used to form aerial barrages around important locations. Almost 1,500 balloons were in use at the height of the Battle. Many members of the Women's Auxiliary Air Force worked for Balloon Command. The deflated balloon was carried on the back of a lorry. A winch was used to raise and lower the balloon.

Ordinary men and women were trained to work in Britain's Home Forces, in anti-aircraft batteries or operating barrage balloons. Others worked long hours on top of their demanding regular jobs as air raid wardens, auxiliary fire fighters and first aiders.

3.7-inch anti-aircraft gun

The 3.7 entered service in 1938. This mobile gun was set up in groups, usually of four, together with equipment that gave the crew information on the height and expected position of enemy aircraft.

During the Blitz it took thousands of shells to destroy an enemy aircraft. But by 1944, with the introduction of radar, it took only 150 to bring down a V1 flying bomb. By this time, many of the gun sites were manned by Home Guardsmen and women from the Auxiliary Territorial Service.

Above Left Members of the Women's Auxiliary Air Force (WAAF) learning how to handle a barrage balloon
IWM CH 7346

Above The 3.7-inch anti-aircraft gun in action
IWM TR 450

Left St Paul's Cathedral during a German raid, December 1941
IWM HU 36220A, courtesy of the *Daily Mail*

Nash ambulance

Air Raid Precautions (ARP) services were set up in 1937 in anticipation of heavy air raids and casualties. First aid parties, posts and the emergency Ambulance Service formed an important part of the ARP arrangements.

Many vehicles were converted for use as ambulances. The American Nash Ambassador car in *Battle of Britain* was converted by Thomas Bata for use at his shoe factory in East Tilbury, London, in 1939.

Austin K2 National Fire Service truck

The K2 was a pre-war commercial design. Many like this 1942 example were built for war service. The K2 carried 12 fire fighters and towed a water pump.

German bombers returned to Britain in 1942 and again in 1944, but with less effect. Then in June 1944, the UK was attacked by a new German weapon, the V1 pilotless flying bomb. V2 rockets followed from 7 September. They were bigger, faster and more accurate than V1s. Their approach was silent, and their huge explosive force could be felt for miles beyond the immediate impact area. V1s and V2s killed almost 9,000 civilians, but the attacks came too late to change the course of the war.

At its peak wartime strength, RAF Fighter Command had over 100 squadrons. But when the war ended in 1945, the RAF was reduced in size: by 1948, it possessed just over 200 front line aircraft in 25 squadrons. Air defence soon became a priority again, however, as Britain faced new threats and technologies in the Cold War.

Top The Nash ambulance and Austin K2 National Fire Service truck
Courtesy of Peter Dousek

Above The V1 flying bomb, sometimes called a 'Doodlebug', in flight
IWM CL 3433

Right A warden with a child rescued from a house destroyed by a V1
IWM HU 36227, courtesy of Topfoto

Gloster Meteor F8

The Meteor was Britain's first jet fighter and the only Allied jet to see operational service during the Second World War. It had some success against V1s in July 1944.

Improved versions of the Meteor followed after the war. The F8 entered service in 1950, replacing the earlier F4 as the mainstay of Fighter Command's Home Defence Squadrons. Duxford's Meteor WK991 served with No. 56 Squadron in the late 1950s.

RAF Fighter Command responded to the threat of Soviet Russia's bombers and nuclear weapons in the 1950s by expanding to 600 aircraft. Many of these were jet-powered fighters armed with air-to-air missiles. Operational centres were moved underground, and radar systems improved. Surface-to-air missiles were also introduced, and by the 1960s the Lightning, the RAF's first supersonic fighter, had entered service. Many of these measures, however, would only have been effective in a conventional war. They could do little to prevent a Soviet nuclear missile strike, which could not be countered with traditional forms of air defence. Instead, Britain relied on the deterrent effect of the RAF's nuclear V bombers, and later on the Navy's nuclear-missile-carrying submarines.

Above Left The Gloster Meteor in *Battle of Britain*
Courtesy of Peter Dousek

Above The Bloodhound missile, a variant of which is on display in *Battle of Britain*, was designed to shoot down enemy bombers
IWM RAF-T 718

Below Hawker Hunters in flight
IWM RAF-T 9

Hawker Hunter F6

The Hunter was probably the most successful British post-war combat aircraft and was the standard RAF fighter of the 1950s. It replaced the Meteor F8 and served until the introduction of the Lightning in the early 1960s.

The Duxford Hunter, XE627, was built by the Hawker Aircraft Company in 1956. It joined No. 65 Squadron at RAF Duxford in November 1956. It remained with the unit until August 1961.

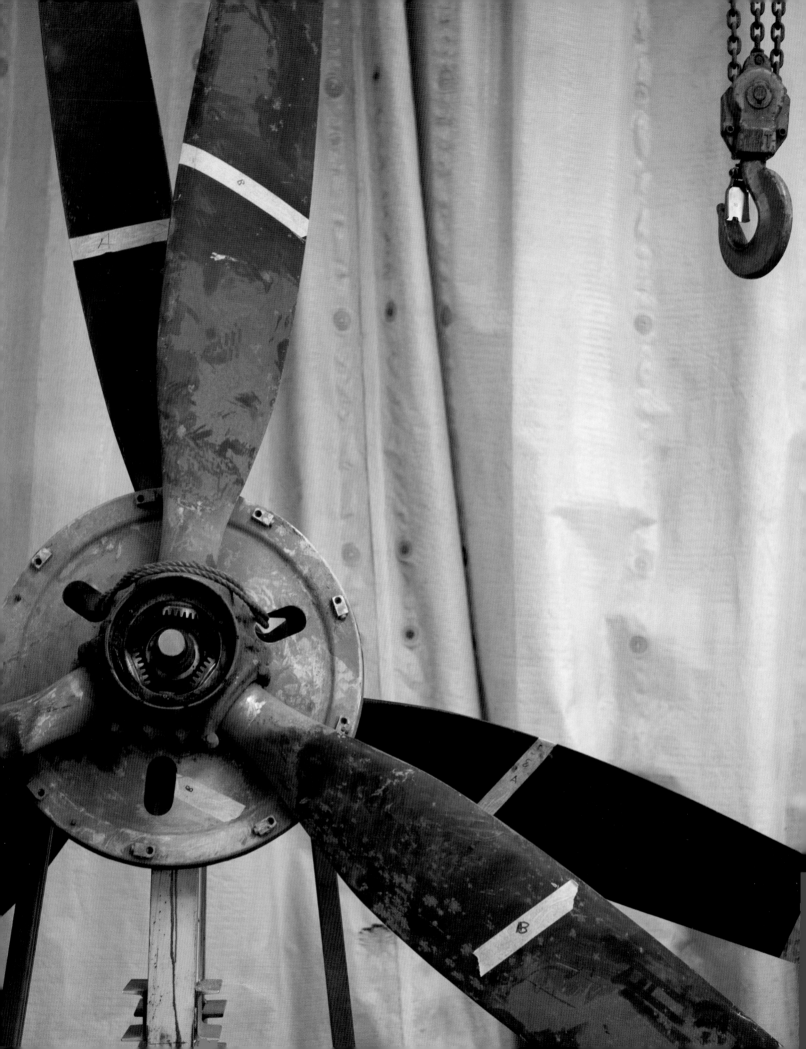

Conservation in Action

A team of dedicated staff and volunteers at IWM Duxford care for hundreds of IWM's most significant exhibits. The techniques and materials used to preserve a First World War aircraft are very different from those required for a modern military jet, but each must be carefully looked after if it is to be available for future generations to see. Much of this vital work is carried out in full view of visitors.

Exhibits receive attention in different ways. Conservation is maintaining an aircraft in its present state to prevent future deterioration. Restoration is returning an aircraft to a complete, historically accurate condition. Much of the work carried out at IWM Duxford is conservation.

Although aircraft and vehicles may seem durable, they are in fact surprisingly delicate. For example, many historic military aircraft were not expected to have a long life, so were not always built to last. All of the materials used in aircraft construction are vulnerable. Wood and fabric will rot and decay, and metal will corrode if left untreated.

The Conservation staff and volunteers fix the effects of existing decay and corrosion, but they also work hard to prevent the future deterioration of historic aircraft. This often involves the complete dismantling and strip-down of an aircraft, so that internal corrosion or damage can be treated, before reassembling the exhibit.

Top A Conservation Officer works on the Airspeed Oxford
IWM DUX_2005_054_002

Above A volunteer inspects part of the Vulcan
IWM DUX_2004_066_01

Left Many of the tanks and vehicles in and around *Land Warfare* are maintained in running condition
IWM DUX_2007_045_025

Restoration and conservation is undertaken in several stages. The task is assessed, the exhibit's original condition recorded, the paint carefully removed to reveal underlying colour schemes and damaged parts are removed for repair or replacement. Severely corroded or decayed areas are repaired if possible, but if beyond repair they are replaced. Less severe corrosion to metal areas is removed by mechanical or chemical means, and hidden areas are covered with suitable preservatives. Engines, if still installed, are also conserved before reassembly begins. Then, the exhibits are painted in historically appropriate colour schemes.

Once an aircraft or vehicle is ready for display, it must be looked after in the proper environmental conditions. High light levels, high relative humidity (the amount of moisture in the air), changing heat levels and vigorous cleaning can all cause serious damage. Therefore, IWM Duxford uses technology such as dehumidifiers to create carefully controlled indoor environments for its aircraft and other exhibits.

Restoring TSR2

Duxford's British Aircraft Corporation TSR2 was still on the production line when the project was cancelled in 1965. It therefore had many panels and parts missing. After spending several subsequent years outside, it was clear that a major conservation project was necessary to preserve this landmark airframe.

The first stage was to strip off all the existing paint so that the Conservation team could carry out a thorough condition survey. They then knew exactly what work was needed.

The second stage was to repair the corrosion damage and to manufacture the missing panels. Some of these panels were originally made of composite fibre, so these were replicated as accurately as possible using fibreglass resin.

The third stage was to repaint the aircraft, paying particular attention to the accuracy of the various stencils and markings.

Top After lengthy conservation, the Canberra is suspended in *AirSpace*
IWM DUX_2006_033_247

Above Conserving the RE8
IWM DUX_2005_031_002

Right Conserving TSR2
IWM DUX_2005_047_026

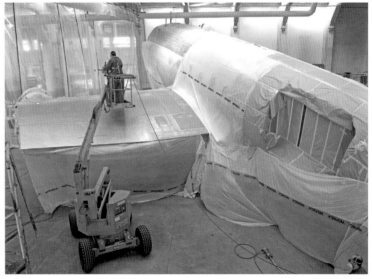

Top Re-covering the wings
of the Swordfish
IWM DUX_2004_029_006

Left The Harrier undergoes
full conservation
IWM DUX_2004_056_008

Above Respraying the Hastings
in the spray bay
IWM DUX_2007_019_008

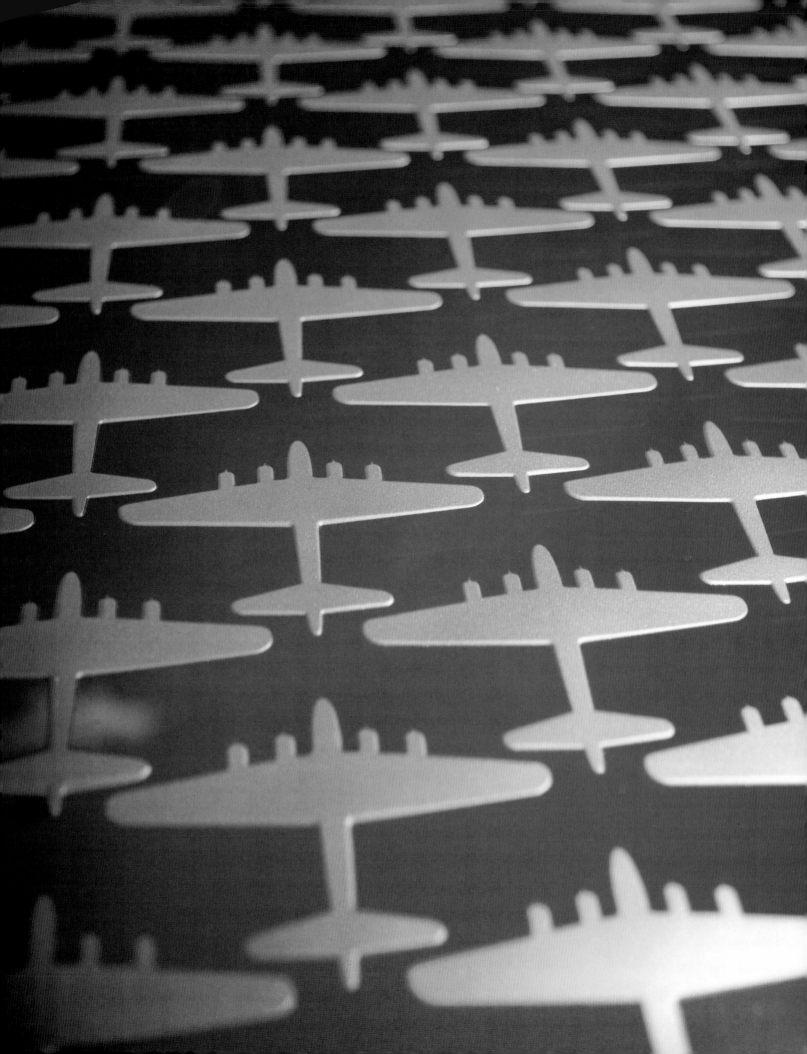

American Air Museum

The *American Air Museum*, designed by the internationally famous architect Lord Foster, stands as a memorial to the 26,000 US airmen who gave their lives while flying from British bases, including Duxford, during the Second World War. It exhibits the finest collection of American combat aircraft outside of the United States. It tells the story of American air power, its effect on the modern world and the Second World War in Europe in particular.

Above The *American Air Museum* in Britain
IWM SITE DUX_000333

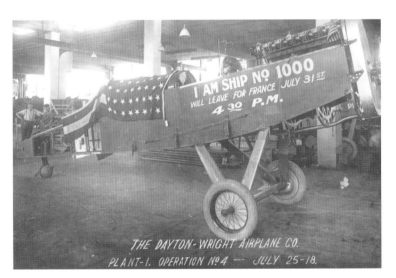

In 1916, the United States produced only 400 aeroplanes. Yet between April 1917, when America entered the First World War, and the end of the war in November 1918, the US manufactured 11,000 aircraft. The US Army Air Service also grew massively. By 1918, it had 195,000 men operating 3,500 aircraft in Europe. The US emerged from the war as a world power that had demonstrated both its industrial might and its huge military potential.

Liberty V12 aero engine

The Liberty was the world's first mass-produced aircraft engine. The American aircraft industry mainly built European designs under licence during the First World War.

The British DH4 bomber was one of the American built types powered by the Liberty, a hastily designed but effective liquid cooled engine made by the car manufacturers. By the end of the war, 15,600 had been built. The DH4 was the only American built aircraft to operate on the Western Front.

Above Left The 1,000th DH4 built at Dayton, Ohio, 1918
National Air and Space Museum, Smithsonian Institution (SI 81-3527)

Left A Liberty-engined DH4 of the 166th Aero Squadron
US AirForce (USAF 121803AC) via National Air and Space Museum, Smithsonian Institution

Above American servicemen outside King's College chapel, Cambridge
The Cambridgeshire Collection

Right Improving Anglo-American relations at a dance
IWM D 14124

American civil aviation grew rapidly between the wars, while military aviation lagged behind. In 1939, one American general described the US air forces as 'fifth-rate', but by the end of the Second World War in 1945, the US had been transformed into the world's leading air power. In the spring of 1944, the US 8th and 9th Air Forces occupied over 120 airfields in the UK, with half a million personnel and over 9,000 aircraft. The largest concentration was in East Anglia, where their presence had an enormous social impact. The US 8th Air Force partnered RAF Bomber Command in a combined bomber offensive designed to destroy Germany's war effort. The US 9th Air Force provided support for ground forces in north-west Europe. Together, they made a decisive contribution to the Allied victory in the war. But the cost was high; over 80,000 Allied airmen and 600,000 German civilians lost their lives.

Left American servicemen in a traditional British pub
Courtesy of A C Sloan

By the time the US 8th Air Force was approaching its peak strength in 1944, 300 new aircraft were being completed each day by American aircraft factories. From 1939 to 1945, the US built some 325,000 aircraft, a total greater than the combined production of Britain, Germany and Japan. Some 36,000 of these were costly four-engine bombers and transports. The US 8th Air Force flew the Boeing B17 Flying Fortress and the Consolidated B24 Liberator heavy bombers on daylight raids over Germany and occupied Europe. Twenty thousand men in 3,000 bombers and their supporting fighters, flying from up to 59 airfields, could be involved in a single day's action.

Boeing B17G Flying Fortress

The B17 is the best-known American bomber of the Second World War. With its armament of 13 machine guns, it flew in massive defensive formations, but effective German fighter attacks showed these to be ineffective until the introduction of long-range P51 fighters, which could fly with the bombers all the way to their targets.

The *American Air Museum* B17 is serial 44-83735, built in 1945 and delivered too late to see war service.

Douglas C47 Skytrain

The C47 was the military version of the DC3, which first flew in 1935. It was the most successful and widely used military transport aircraft of the Second World War. C47s were also used to carry parachutists, to evacuate casualties and to tow gliders. Over 2,000 were used in support of the Allied invasion of Europe in June 1944.

The C47 in the *American Air Museum* served with the 316th Troop Carrier Group, US 9th Air Force and it participated in the Normandy landing in June 1944, the airborne assault on the Netherlands in September 1944 and the crossing of the Rhine in March 1945.

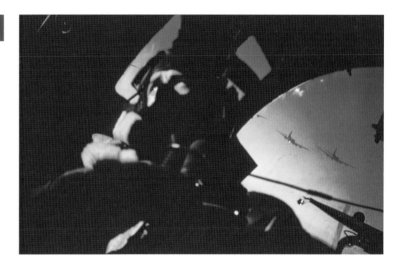

Above A B17 crewman
Courtesy of Paul Chryst

Above The B24 Liberator
IWM DUX_2003_10_14

Left A C47 glider-tug about to pick up a Waco CG4A transport glider
National Air and Space Museum
(NASM2A28839), Smithsonian Institution

Bomber missions took three to eleven hours. Crews flew in a dangerous, freezing, vibrating, deafening environment. But each crewman was part of a ten or twelve-man team, bound together by camaraderie in the face of great danger. Initially, US fighters did not have enough range to stay with the bombers all the way to their targets. In the first year of operations, only 36 per cent of heavy bomber airmen had a chance of completing a 25-mission tour. The fighter pilot's experience of war was one of lonely fatigue, strapped in a small noisy cockpit for three to seven hours on long bomber escort missions.

Republic P47D Thunderbolt

The P47 was the main escort fighter of the 8th Air Force from spring 1943 to early 1944. Its limited range was extended by the use of drop tanks, but it was phased out of the escort role when the P51 Mustang became available. However, the P47 was a rugged aircraft, and it continued in the ground attack role with the 9th Air Force.

This P47 is displayed in the marking of Colonel Hubert Zemke's *Oregon's Britannia*. Zemke was the commander of the top scoring 56th Fighter Group.

The war in the Pacific against Japan was won thanks to the US Navy's dominance at sea and naval air power. Carrier-based dive-bomber and torpedo aircraft could destroy an enemy at distances far greater than battleships. With the threat of the Japanese navy removed in a string of victories mainly decided by aircraft, US Navy carriers could support amphibious landings and ultimately launch raids on Japan itself. These successes inspired the development of modern carrier groups armed with nuclear weapons.

Top The *American Air Museum*'s P47, painted in the markings of the 56th Fighter Group
IWM DUX_1997_0001_0724

Above The Mustang could also operate as a fighter-bomber
USAF

Grumman TBM3 Avenger

The Avenger was the standard US Navy carrier-based torpedo bomber in service from mid 1942. It was the first single-engine American aircraft to have a power-operated gun turret, and the first to carry the heavy 22-inch torpedo. It could also carry bombs, rockets and depth charges.

This Avenger is painted to represent the TBM flown by President George Bush Sr when he was a Lieutenant in the US Navy in the Pacific in 1944. He named the aircraft after his wife, Barbara.

Left US Navy Grumman Avengers prepare for take-off
IWM NYF 40315

In 1945, armed with B29 strategic bombers, the US 20th Air Force attacked Japan. The effects were devastating. Japan's economy was shattered; civilian casualties exceeded 800,000, including 300,000 dead, and millions were made homeless. But Japan continued to fight on. Then, on 6 August 1945, a single atomic bomb was dropped by the B29 *Enola Gay* on Hiroshima, killing 80,000 people. A second bomb was dropped on Nagasaki on 9 August killing another 35,000. Japan surrendered, bringing the Second World War to an end, the bomber was confirmed as a decisive weapon and the world entered the nuclear age.

Boeing B29 Superfortress

With its long range, partly pressurised fuselage and remote controlled gun turrets, the B29 was the most advanced bomber produced in the Second World War. It was used in the strategic bombing of Japan and in the early years of the Cold War when it was the main USAF nuclear deterrent.

B29A-BN, serial number 44-61748, was built in 1944 and served with several USAAF and USAF units. During the Korean War it was with the 7th Bomb Wing and flew bombing raids against communications targets.

In the 1940s, aircraft were the only means of delivering nuclear bombs. To act as a deterrent against Soviet attacks during the subsequent 'Cold War', US air power was expanded with the introduction of jet aircraft capable of carrying nuclear weapons. The US Air Force (USAF) became independent of the US Army and Navy in 1947. Then, its Strategic Air Command (SAC) had fewer than 300 aircraft, but by the end of the 1950s it had more than 1,800 long-range jet bombers. Deployed to bases in Western Europe, including the United Kingdom, and to the Far East, American bombers demonstrated the willingness of the United States to protect its interests and allies world wide. With the introduction of long-range missiles in the 1960s, the US bomber force was reduced, and after the end of the Cold War, fell to fewer than 200.

Boeing B52D Stratofortress

The B52 has been the mainstay of USAF strategic bombing capability since 1955, and it is expected to serve in that capacity until 2030. The B52 was capable of bombing the Soviet Union from bases in the US, and part of their force was always kept on alert, able to be airborne within 15 minutes. In 1991, America declared the Cold War over by ordering this capability to be stood down.

B52D, serial number 56-0689, was built in 1956 and was delivered to the 28th Bomb Wing USAF in October 1957. During the Vietnam War, '689 took part in 200 missions.

Left B29s of 21st US Bomber Command during the Second World War
IWM NYP 69366

Above Duxford's B52 arrives in October 1983
IWM 1983_0043_0031

The Cuban Missile Crisis took the world to the brink of a nuclear war. In October 1962, American U2 spy planes revealed Soviet medium-range missiles were being installed on the Caribbean island of Cuba, less than 400 km (248 miles) from the US. America demanded their removal. US forces were put on full alert, and nuclear bombers were kept in the air. The Soviets withdrew their missiles, and in a reciprocal move, the US removed missiles from Turkey. Although both superpowers realised how close they came to war, the Cold War and its associated arms race continued.

Lockheed SR71A Blackbird

In 1958, the Lockheed Advanced Development Projects 'Skunk Works' began work on a successor to the U2 'spyplane'. The Blackbird's first flight was in 1962, and it served with USAF from 1968 to 1997 as a strategic reconnaissance aircraft. With a maximum speed of 3,529 km/h (2,193 mph), the SR71 was the highest flying and fastest jet aeroplane.

This aircraft first flew in April 1996. Among the bases it operated from was RAF Mildenhall in the UK. It set the current altitude record for horizontal flight at 25,929 m (85,069 ft) in 1976.

Superpower rivalry also fuelled regional wars. Two of these, the Korean War and the Vietnam War, developed into major conflicts involving US forces and the use of air power on a massive scale. However, in Vietnam in particular, air power did not prove to be a decisive factor.

Above A Lockheed SR71 Blackbird is prepared for flight
USAF

Bell UH1 Huey

The Huey was the famous 'workhorse' helicopter of the Vietnam War. Helicopters allowed the Americans to reinforce surrounded positions and to move troops quickly. But they may also have contributed to the illusion that the war could be won by air power alone.

The Berlin Airlift of 1948–1949 saw the return of US bombers to British bases. The US 3rd Air Force was formed in 1951 to command tactical air units in the UK. By the late 1950s, the USAF had 16 airfields, another dozen on standby and some 40,000 personnel in Britain. In the 1970s and 1980s, the USAF NATO commitment was three fighter-bomber wings and one reconnaissance wing. More recently, USAF UK-based aircraft and personnel have served in the Gulf War of 1991, Serbia and Kosovo in 1999 and in Iraq. With the fall of the Berlin Wall and the collapse of the Soviet Union, USAF units in the UK have been significantly reduced.

Above A Huey moves troops of the 1st Cavalry Division (Air-mobile) into action in February 1966
IWM CT 152

General Dynamics F111E

The F111 was the world's first swing-wing combat aircraft, used by the USAF from the Vietnam era to the Gulf War. It was a rugged long-range strike aircraft capable of delivering conventional or nuclear weapons from low altitude.

F111s were based in the UK at RAF Upper Heyford with the 20th Fighter Wing, and at RAF Lakenheath with the 48th Fighter Wing. This aircraft, serial number 67-0120, flew 19 missions with the 77th Fighter Squadron (20th FW) during the Gulf War.

Left USAF F111 Aardvarks returning from a mission during the 1991 Gulf War
IWM GLF 1110

Land Warfare

Over the course of the twentieth century, the mechanisation of warfare has altered forever the way battles are fought, won and lost. From the awesome artillery barrages of the First World War, through the giant tank battles of the Second World War, to the high-speed mechanised conflict of today, the exhibitions in *Land Warfare* chart the nature of this change.

Above The Queen's Bays cavalry, after an action
IWM Q 51484

Below The Battle of Morval, September 1916. Supporting troops scramble out of their trenches to go forward near Ginchy, France
IWM Q 1309

Bottom The American FWD General Service Truck
IWM N_1, courtesy of Reeve Photography

Before the First World War, the main method of getting to battle was on foot. Infantry marched and cavalry rode. Transport was horse-drawn, and there were few mechanised vehicles in military use. By the outbreak of war in 1914, cavalry and infantry were still riding and marching to war. Artillery was horse-drawn. Some guns were designed to fight side-by-side with infantry, and some guns were kept further back, to support set-piece battles.

When the First World War began, both sides attempted to outflank each other in France. The front line soon stretched from Switzerland to the Channel coast. Faced with a hail of fire from rifles and machine guns, both sides dug in. By the end of 1915, the lines were set, and over the next three years they rarely moved more than ten miles. Over this period, however, the use of motor-transport increased enormously, sometimes to move troops, but most often to tow artillery pieces.

American FWD, 3-ton General Service Truck

The four-wheel drive FWD truck was a US commercial vehicle supplied to the Allies from 1915. It was most frequently used as an artillery-towing vehicle or tractor.

On the Western Front, FWDs were used for many tasks, including repair shops, balloon winches and searchlight trucks, but it was in the hauling of bulky stores, and particularly in towing large artillery pieces, that the FWD excelled. By 1918, the British army had 3,000 of these vehicles in service. The FWD remained in service until 1930.

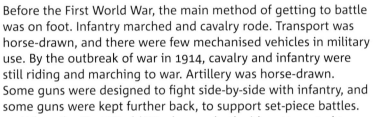

Both sides tried to end the deadlock, first by bombarding the enemy with bigger guns and more shells. This led to massive 'rail guns', huge weapons that moved around on tracks. As the war progressed, better methods of communication and control were developed, and the use of aircraft for spotting helped improve the accuracy of the guns. This was not enough, however, to break the stalemate.

Tanks were invented to do just that. Developed simultaneously by the French and British, their job was to cross no man's land in relative safety, unhindered by fortifications and barbed wire. They offered protection for the advancing infantry. Although the appearance of tanks on the battlefield initially over-awed the Germans, they soon found their weak spots. Tanks were slow, unreliable and vulnerable to direct artillery hits. They did not greatly influence the outcome of the war, which ended in 1918 thanks to a combination of factors: the dramatically improved fighting ability of the British Army, the exhaustion of the German military machine after four years of Allied naval blockade and the arrival of American troops.

The First World War showed that warfare and mechanisation were now inextricably linked. In the inter-war period, development slowed, as the world recovered from four years of devastating conflict. Traditional military officers wanted to return to pre-1914 methods and forget the horror and deadlock of trench warfare. But there were a few forward-thinking officers, particularly in the German army, who saw the possibilities and advantages of further mechanisation.

British 6-inch Heavy Howitzer

This weapon was of late 19th century design and continued to be used during the First World War. The howitzer on display was issued in 1898 and served in the Boer War, 1898–1902.

It was sent to France in 1915, where it is believed to have served on the Neuve-Chappelle-Loos front between June 1915 and February 1916, firing a total of 1,697 rounds.

Right The British 6-inch Heavy Howitzer
IWM DUX_2008_006_010

Below A convoy of British lorries on the road near Carnoy, France, during the Battle of the Somme, 1916
IWM Q 1435

German Panzerkampfwagen IV Ausf. B Tank

The Panzer IV became the backbone of German armoured divisions on all fronts during the Second World War.

Intended to be an infantry support vehicle, the Panzer IV was modified to become Germany's main battle tank. Over 8,000 were produced. The type was used in the invasion of Poland, France, the Balkans and Russia. It was regularly updated and modified until the end of the war.

When the Second World War began, the armies on all sides were equipped with a mix of modern and vintage weaponry. Germany utilised modern mechanised warfare ideas best, in the form of 'Blitzkrieg' (Lightning War). The theory was based on the tank as part of an all-arms team, the Panzer Division. Aircraft such as the Stuka dive-bomber, operating as 'aerial artillery', would blast enemy defences. Then, the tanks would smash through at a selected point, quickly followed by mechanised infantry (troops in vehicles, rather than on foot) and support arms, such as anti-aircraft guns.

Against this tactic, the Allies were largely powerless. As the Germans swept through the Low Countries and France, only the retreat to Dunkirk saved the British Army from annihilation in 1940.

Once the RAF had won the Battle of Britain, and the threat of a German invasion had receded, the British decided to go on the offensive. The only place that Axis forces could be effectively challenged in late 1940 was North Africa. Attacking a large but poorly equipped Italian army, British forces won a series of victories until the Germans sent reinforcements under the command of General Erwin Rommel, equipped with tanks such as the Panzer IV.

Left The Panzer IV

IWM Duxford, Interpretation Department

Advantage see-sawed between the Axis (German and Italian) and Allied forces in North Africa until the battle of El Alamein in October and November 1942, masterminded by General Bernard Montgomery. Victory in this battle, combined with British and American landings in French Morocco and Algeria, forced the Germans to surrender in May 1943. Allied success was due in part to new tanks, such as the M4 Sherman. Though it was slightly inferior to the Panzer IV on the battlefield, it was easier to produce and simpler to maintain.

Sherman Grizzly Tank

The Sherman Grizzly was a Canadian-built version of the US Sherman tank. Shermans were produced in huge numbers. They were by far the most common tank in the armoury of the Western Allies and saw action with every Allied army on every front.

Though not the best tank of the war, the Sherman was simple to build, easy to maintain, reliable and rugged.

The Allied invasion of Italy, launched in 1943 at the insistence of Churchill, was designed to attack Axis Europe's 'soft underbelly'. Italy surrendered quickly, but the Germans refused to give up their former ally's territory. Fighting was particularly fierce in terrain dominated by mountains and rivers, and infantry and artillery, not tanks, dominated the struggle.

When the Nazis invaded the Soviet Union in June 1941, their rapid Blitzkrieg offensive threatened to crush Russian resistance. It was the ultimate use of mechanised warfare: the Germans advanced over 600 km (378 miles) in barely three months. Soviet forces proved to be no match for the German tactics in these early stages. But the Russians soon showed that they had some very powerful tanks, particularly the T34. In response, the German army introduced new tanks of their own, such as the Panzer VI Tiger.

Soviet T34/85 Medium Tank

The T34 was arguably the finest tank design of its time, thanks to its combination of thick, angled armour, heavy firepower and superb mobility.

Of all the tanks the German Army encountered in the Second World War, the T34 presented the biggest challenge. Between 1940 and 1945, a total of 64,558 T34 tanks were built. In the same period, German tank production totalled 26,000. The successful T34 remained in production after the war. It can still be found in service around the world, due to its robust nature and easy maintenance.

Top British and Australian troops at El Alamein in July 1942
IWM E 14306

Middle A Canadian Sherman tank in the ruins of the French town of Caen
IWM NYT 1297E

Bottom The T34/85 tank
IWM Duxford, Interpretation Department

Above Canadian troops go ashore
on Juno beach, 6 June 1944
IWM A 23938

A combination of harsh conditions and dogged Soviet resistance turned the tide in the East. And by 1943, the Red Army had learnt the hard way how to use its tanks properly. Also, the tank factories, relocated as the Russians had retreated in 1941 and 1942, were now producing excellent vehicles in quantities the Germans could never hope to match. After the bloody battle of Stalingrad and the largest tank battle ever, at Kursk in 1943, the Soviets began to force the Germans to retreat.

D-Day, the Allied invasion of north-west Europe, took place on 6 June 1944, and was the largest seaborne invasion ever mounted. Under cover of aircraft and naval bombardment, an Allied army landed on the beaches of Normandy, France, breaking into Hitler's 'Fortress Europe'. At first the Germans were caught off balance, then fought back strongly. Eventually the Allies broke German resistance, and over the following months began to push them out of France. They faced several setbacks, including the devastating annihilation of the British 1st Airborne Division at Arnhem, Holland, and a German counter-offensive in the Ardennes. But with Allied forces advancing in the west and the east, Germany could not avoid defeat and surrendered in May 1945.

Above Special 'Mulberry' harbours were used after D-Day to allow armoured vehicles to be brought ashore more efficiently
IWM BU 1024

The Montgomery Caravans

This three-vehicle mobile tactical headquarters was used by Field Marshal Montgomery throughout the campaign in north-west Europe. 'Monty' is the best-known British Army commander of the Second World War.

The first caravan, captured from the Italians, was his only home from August 1942 to May 1943. When a second caravan was captured, the first vehicle became Monty's office, and the second was used as his bedroom until the end of the war in Europe.

The map lorry was built to the designs of Monty's personal staff. It became the nerve centre of Monty's tactical headquarters from June 1944 to the German surrender, and its interior has remained largely unaltered since Victory in Europe (VE) Day.

Above Montgomery in his map caravan with King George VI, 1944
IWM TR 2393

The war against Japan in the Pacific and Far East took longer to complete and was fought with gruelling intensity between the Allies and the Japanese. It raged over vast distances and in extremes of climate and geography. After their stunning attack on Pearl Harbor in 1941, the Japanese won a succession of victories as they overran territory formerly controlled by Western countries. Then, from June 1942, the Allies checked the Japanese advance, went onto the offensive and took the war to Japan itself. The Japanese proved a ferocious enemy and treated captured prisoners of war with appalling brutality.

Left Sikh troops clear a Japanese foxhole at Mandalay
IWM IND 4550

After the war, tanks and armoured fighting vehicles continued to be the mainstay of the armed forces. The onset of the Cold War in the late 1940s meant that the West now faced the threat of the enormous Soviet army. To counter this, Britain maintained a standing army in Germany, the British Army of the Rhine (BAOR), as part of the North Atlantic Treaty Organisation (NATO). For 45 years this force trained for a war that did not happen. Each side attempted to produce tanks, weapons and vehicles that would outperform the enemy's. Integral to British forces were tanks such as the Centurion and Chieftain, kept ready to defend West Germany in particular from the threat of massive Soviet invasion.

This NATO commitment had a profound effect on British policy outside Europe. In the face of economic pressures, and as former colonies gained their independence, Britain's military presence outside Europe steadily declined. But withdrawal from the Empire was not in all cases a peaceful process. As a consequence, the British Army was drawn into a variety of police actions, anti-terrorist campaigns and smaller wars in the post-Second World War period.

From 1950 to 1953, British and Commonwealth forces fought in Korea as part of a United Nations force against North Korean and Chinese communists. Other operations saw British land forces involvement. These included counter-insurgency actions in Malaya, Borneo and Aden, and closer to home, anti-terrorist activities in Northern Ireland. In 1982, British troops successfully liberated the Falkland Islands after they were invaded by Argentina.

Centurion main battle tank

The Centurion was the first British post-war main battle tank. It proved to be a very successful design and was used in significant numbers in the Korean War, 1951-1953. The Centurion was upgraded several times in the 1950s with the addition of thicker armour and better weapons.

The Centurion in *Land Warfare* entered service in 1952 and was used as a training vehicle in the late 1950s.

Above A Daimler Ferret scout car of the 1st King's Dragoon Guards in Malaya, 1957
IWM D 88417

Top Right The Centurion
Courtesy of Peter Dousek

Right British Royal Marines in the Falklands, 1982. Although troops had some access to ground and air transport, several battles involved lengthy marches over inhospitable terrain.
IWM FKD 2028

Above British Challenger tanks wait to go into action during the 1991 Gulf War
IWM GLF 472

Left Four Iraqi BMP-1 armoured personnel carriers destroyed in the Euphrates River valley during Operation 'Desert Storm'. US Department of Defence photo taken by SSgt Dean Wagner on 4 March 1991.

Soviet BMP-1 Mechanised Infantry Combat Vehicle

The BMP-1 was designed to carry troops into combat, and also to allow them to fight from within the vehicle. This is why it is fitted with rifle ports along each side. Developed for use with the Soviet Army, the type was also widely exported. The BMP-1 in *Land Warfare* was operated by the Iraqi army. It was captured by British forces in the Gulf War, 1991.

In 1991 the British Army again fought under the auspices of the United Nations in the Gulf. Throughout the 1990s, British troops were involved in other UN and NATO peacekeeping missions, such as Bosnia. In the early 2000s, British land forces saw action in Afghanistan and Iraq. While the vehicles used in these recent conflicts are technologically very different to those of a hundred years ago, the courage of the soldiers who use them has remained constant.

Above The GKN Saxon
IWM

GKN Saxon (Internal Security) Patrol Vehicle

The Saxon was designed to be used as a 'battle-taxi', to transport troops into a combat area but not to act as a fighting vehicle. First used in the 1980s, Saxons have been used in several conflicts, including Bosnia, Iraq and Afghanistan. The 'Patrol' variant carries extra protection against rocket-propelled grenades, a weapon often used by enemy forces such as the Taliban. The Saxon in *Land Warfare* served with the British Army in Afghanistan from 2007 – 2010.

The Royal Anglian Regiment Museum

The Royal Anglian Regiment is the infantry regiment of East Anglia and the East Midlands.

The Regiment was formed in 1964, after a series of amalgamations. Between 1958 and 1960, the East Anglian Regiments succeeded the former county regiments of Norfolk, Lincolnshire, Suffolk, Cambridgeshire, Bedfordshire, Hertfordshire, Leicestershire, Essex and Northamptonshire, which were mostly raised between 1685 and 1755.

The Royal Anglian Regiment Museum collection covers the history of the East Anglian Regiments and the Royal Anglian Regiment. The Museum office, archive and exhibition gallery are based at IWM Duxford.

Archive material is available to researchers within the Museum office, while the gallery in *Land Warfare* depicts the life of a modern infantry regiment and its soldiers. Exhibits include Regimental Colours, silverware, interactive displays and tableaux, along with uniforms, medals and equipment from the Regiment's many deployments, including Malaya, Aden, Germany, Northern Ireland, Bosnia, Iraq and Afghanistan.

Activity sheets enable younger visitors to learn more about the Regiment, and a number of events are held by the Museum during the year, at which visitors have the opportunity to talk to veterans of the Regiment about their experiences of Army life.

The Museum can be accessed online at royalanglianmuseum.org.uk.

Top Operation Lastay Kulang, 1st Battalion, Afghanistan, 2007

Above The Royal Anglian Regiment Museum Gallery in *Land Warfare*

The Cambridgeshire Regiment Exhibition

Located next to the Royal Anglian Regiment Museum gallery, this display tells the story of the Cambridgeshire Regiment, from its origins in 1860 as the Cambridgeshire Rifle Volunteer Corps to its last manifestation as D (Cambridgeshire) Company, 6th Volunteer Battalion, The Royal Anglian Regiment.

Many of the objects on display testify to the unique and distinguished history of this regiment, which remarkably has been manned by part-time soldiers who have time and time again shown themselves to be every bit as professional as their full-time counterparts.

During the First World War, the soldiers of the 1/1st Battalion, The Cambridgeshire Regiment, won over 300 gallantry awards, including 42 for a single action: the assault on the Schwaben Redoubt in 1916.

Above This attack on the Schwaben Redoubt by men of the Cambridgeshire Regiment was described by Field Marshal Haig as 'One of the finest feats of arms in the history of the British Army'

The Cambridgeshire Regiment Collection

Learning

IWM Duxford has a dedicated Department for Learning. The aim is to provide an engaging experience for formal and informal learners of all ages.

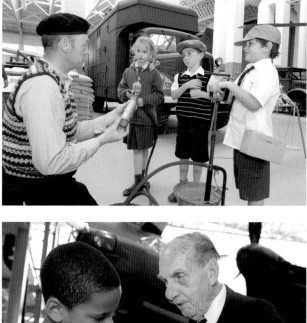

Approximately 50,000 formal learners visit IWM Duxford each year from primary and secondary schools and colleges. Talks and activities offered relate to History, Literacy, Citizenship, Science, Technology, Engineering and Mathematics. Also very popular are role play sessions and 'People's Stories' workshops, which take place amongst the exhibits for maximum impact. A short description of all the activities available for schools and colleges can be found on the website. Museum staff are happy to adapt talks to suit the needs of particular groups.

Teachers can take advantage of free preliminary visits in order to plan their trip and staff in the department are happy to advise on options according to the age of the children, the Programme of Study and the time available.

There are resources on the website to support the self-directed part of the visit.

For informal learners the department offers daily introductory tours, taster talks and weekend tours. The introductory tour covers some of the history of Duxford, the museum today and how to make the most of your visit. Taster talks spotlight particular exhibits, and weekend exhibition tours take a more in-depth look at the permanent exhibitions and themes in the hangars. There are special Interest Days and pre-booked tours available on certain dates. These include the Grand Tour, Unseen Duxford, Land Warfare, and Duxford and the Battle of Britain. Please check the website for dates, prices and availability.

Above Learning activities at IWM Duxford

For families the department offers an interactive themed programme every holiday, hands-on activities on Funday Sundays and special family tours. Check the website for details.

Youth groups can have fun exploring IWM Duxford and can use the resources to gain their Air Activities, Basic Aviation Skills and Aeronautics badges. There are prepared activity sheets in the Resources section on the website.

Volunteers make a significant and valuable contribution to the work of the Department for Learning. If you are interested in supporting the offer for formal or informal learners please contact IWM Duxford's Volunteer Co-ordinator.

Telephone the Department for Learning on 01223 499 341, email edu@iwm.org.uk or visit iwm.org.uk for further details on the programme for schools and colleges.

Corporate and Shopping

Selecting the best venue in which to hold your conference, meeting, seminar, or any form of corporate hospitality can go a long way to ensuring that the event is a resounding success. IWM Duxford is proud to offer state of the art facilities and services in an historic setting that will enable your delegates to gain the maximum benefit from your event.

Three remarkable indoor spaces – the breath-taking *AirSpace* **Exhibition Hall**, the **Conservation Hall** and the Foster-designed *American Air Museum* – are available for large-scale hospitality events of up to 700 guests as well as product launches and trade fairs.

Our purpose-built *AirSpace* **Conference Centre** is available for conferences, seminars, meetings, dinners and lunches accommodating up to 200 people. Close proximity to Cambridge, easy access from the M11 motorway and ample free parking add to the Centre's flexibility.

As befitting an historic airfield, we also have a huge variety of outdoor spaces, historic buildings, stunning aircraft and remarkable exhibits, offering endless opportunities for your corporate clients. From entertaining your guests at one of our world-famous air shows to hosting your own outdoor event or providing the perfect location for your photo shoot, IWM Duxford will always leave a lasting impression of excellence.

If you want to get the right results from your next corporate event, please contact the Events Team at duxfordcorporate@iwm.org.uk or call 01223 499 307.

Top Corporate hospitality marquee at one of our Air Shows
IWM Duxford

Above The Conservation Hall in *AirSpace*
IWM Duxford

Below The shop in the Visitor Centre at IWM Duxford
IWM DUX_2008_006_001

There are two shops at IWM Duxford, located in the *American Air Museum* and the Visitor Centre. Enjoy browsing our wide range of books, DVDs, models, prints and posters, learning resources and a large selection of gifts and souvenirs suitable for all ages.

Contact 01223 499 345 for our mail-order service, including trade ordering. Shop online at iwmshop.org.uk.

All purchases support IWM.

Volunteering and Friends of Duxford

Volunteers play an integral part in a wide variety of day-to-day activities at IWM Duxford and are a key element in plans for further improvements. From aircraft conservation to working with the Department for Learning, the volunteers provide an estimated 100,000 hours of work each year.

Above Assisting with a Department for Learning activity
IWM 2010_048_050

There are many different volunteering opportunities at IWM Duxford, some of which are administered by IWM and others by the Duxford Aviation Society (DAS), which is a separate entity to IWM, with full responsibility for its unique collections of civil aircraft and military vehicles. Formed in 1975 the DAS is the largest and most active group of its kind in Britain. Its aims are to acquire, preserve and display British civil aircraft and to work closely with IWM towards the development of IWM Duxford and its collections.

Volunteers can regularly be seen working on the various aircraft, leading guided tours of the site for members of the public and working with families and school groups. It is these individuals who add to the unique and inspirational atmosphere that a visitor will find at IWM Duxford.

Left A volunteer assists with the conservation of the Avro Anson
DXD 2003_005_001

Becoming a Volunteer at IWM Duxford

For an up-to-date list of all the voluntary roles currently available at IWM Duxford, and for information on joining the Duxford Aviation Society, please contact the IWM Duxford Volunteer Co-ordinator for an application pack.

Friends of Duxford

Friends of Duxford is a non-working membership group of DAS, which supports IWM Duxford. Since its creation in 1999 Friends of Duxford has raised over £1 million towards projects such as *AirSpace* and *Historic Duxford*.

As a member of the Friends of Duxford you can become involved with the life of the museum, and further the enjoyment of your visits. Among the benefits are free admission to IWM Duxford on normal opening days, reduced admission tickets for air shows, and the opportunity to participate in exclusive Friends events.

For membership details of both DAS and the Friends of Duxford, please call the Society's office or contact:

Friends of Duxford
IWM Duxford
Cambridgeshire CB22 4QR
Telephone 01223 836 593
iwm.org.uk